Counter-Amores

PHOENIX POETS

JENNIFER CLARVOE

Counter-Amores

THE UNIVERSITY OF CHICAGO PRESS
Chicago & London

JENNIFER CLARVOE is professor of English at Kenyon College and
a recipient of the Rome Prize from the American Academy of Arts and
Letters. She is the author of *Invisible Tender*, winner of the Kate Tufts
Discovery Award and the Poets Out Loud Prize.

The University of Chicago Press, Chicago 60637
The University of Chicago Press, Ltd., London
© 2011 by The University of Chicago
All rights reserved. Published 2011.
Printed in the United States of America
20 19 18 17 16 15 14 13 12 11   1 2 3 4 5

ISBN-13: 978-0-226-10928-2 (paper)
ISBN-10: 0-226-10928-3 (paper)

Library of Congress Cataloging-in-Publication Data
Clarvoe, Jennifer.
    Counter-amores / Jennifer Clarvoe.
        p. cm. — (Phoenix poets)
    ISBN-13: 978-0-226-10928-2 (paper : alk. paper)
    ISBN-10: 0-226-10928-3 (paper : alk. paper)
    I. Title. II. Series: Phoenix poets.
    PS3553.L3444C68 2011
    811'.6—dc22   2010040356

♾ This paper meets the requirements of ANSI/NISO Z39.48-1992
(Permanence of Paper).

Some morning from the boulder-broken beach
He would cry out on life, that what it wants
Is not its own love back in copy speech,
But counter-love, original response.

Robert Frost, "The Most of It"

When training sessions dragged on, Alex would say, "Wanna go
back"— to his cage. More creatively, he'd sometimes announce, "I'm
gonna go away now," and either turn his back on the person work-
ing with him, or sidle as far away as he could get on his perch. "Say
better," he chided the younger parrots that Pepperberg began train-
ing along with him. "You be good, see you tomorrow, I love you,"
he'd say as she left the lab each evening. This was endearing, and the
Times obituary made much of the fact that these were the bird's last
words—although as Anderson points out, it was during such mo-
ments that Alex was, most likely, merely "parroting."

Margaret Talbot, on cognitive scientist Irene Pepperberg and
her parrot, Alex

CONTENTS

ACKNOWLEDGMENTS

Thanks to the editors of the following magazines, where some of these poems first appeared:

The Antioch Review: "After Words," "Counter-Amores 1.2," "Counter-Amores 1.1," and *"Mi Ritrovai"*
Barrow Street: "I Know Why You Went To Memphis, Uh Huh" and "Cultural Instructions: Spring"
The Cincinnati Review: "Counter-Amores 1.5"
Faultline: "The Body is a Disenchanting Thing"
Free Verse: "Island of Opposites," "Words," and "High Time"
The Journal: "Mortal Coil"
Literary Imagination: "After the Equinox" and "Reflecting Pool"
Poetryweb: "A Cradle"
Pool: "In the Nights of Cacophony"
Quadrant: "The Wild Turkeys"
Raritan: "Counter-Amores III.14" and "Counter-Amores III.5"
Slate: "Day of Needs" and "How I Fell & How It Felt"
Southwest Review: "What She Thought"
TriQuarterly: "After the Storm," "Counter-Amores 1.3," and "Counter-Amores 1.7"
The Yale Review: "Bruise"

———

"Counter-Amores III.14" was reprinted in *Conversation Pieces: Poems That Talk to Other Poems,* eds. Kurt Brown and Harold Schechter (New York: Everyman's Library, 2007).

"What She Thought" was reprinted in Verse Daily.

———

The author wishes to express her gratitude to Kenyon College, the Ohio Arts Council, the American Academy of Arts and Letters, and the American Academy in Rome for support that made possible the writing of this book.

I would also like to thank my colleagues, students, and friends at Kenyon College and at the University of California, Irvine, and in the community at the American Academy in Rome.

Special thanks to Linda Bamber, James Cummins, James McMichael, Robert Pinsky, Cammy Thomas, and Stephen Yenser for their critical advice, and to Daniel Bosch for suggesting that I read Ovid's *Amores.*

And thanks to T.

One: Reflecting Pool

AFTER THE EQUINOX

After the Turkish

Can you hear my thirst?
Can you hear it now?

Can you hear a thirst reply
from the opposite hill?

A thirst lies as if sleeping
at the bottom of the valley.

At night it reappears,
pours itself into the dream—

thirst which will swallow thirsts,
as the moon outside will pour

into the bottomless night:
one thirst hoots from its perch,

warning, or invitation,
or the thirsty song of itself.

Another thirst, silent, glides
so low no moon can reach.

3

ISLAND OF OPPOSITES

After a child's drawing

Somewhere in the Ocean of Truth and the Sea of Lies
On carefully labeled tracing paper
Under unlabelled skies,
Equipped, as is proper, with both legend and scale,
Lies the island where we unfold our tale.

To the east, the double-rivers of Upper and Lower Youth
Flow in blue magic marker—
To the west, twin Death
Rivers, too. And a tiny Stream of Disgust
On Withered Hill, amid the shrubs and dust.

Two faces, Janus-like, a pretty girl and a crone,
Appear in the contour intervals,
As if age and ugliness alone
Define what oppositions matter most—
The swampy brow across from the Wisdom Coast.

The labels are written with curlicue flourishes—
A trilling B and C for the Bay of Crime—
Unconscious wishes
That nothing harder oppose us than time?
The tracing paper has yellowed to a shade I'm

Fond of, just as I am of those silly magic markers
(Two shades each of green and blue!)
Neither one so dark as
A rebuke or a threat.
Not yet.

A CRADLE

Woman listening to the sky
releasing the sounds to anyone, everyone, and no one in particular,
it isn't human nature to lie down beneath a thing,
but you can lie down beneath this;

the sky has everything to give, and an unmade bed.
The ferns fall at random, so many golden bear-claws at the roots,
wanton as their fronds, everything opening;
extravagance, *yes*, is the obvious essence of the sky;

the sky is a giver, slow to let go a reluctant sigh.
There are others besides me who have unwrapped themselves from that
    sigh—
whose bodies continue to offer thanks; the birds still wing past them
for their fingertips flourish:

women lift kites, tickled by the notion they might be consecrating a cradle,
and stand still, together—the ribbons of the tails
fluttering apart like milkweed pods as if there were only and everywhere
    birth.

The sheets undo each other in ripples—beautiful over the disparate fluff of
    clouds,
and flare up, gasping, while the sky crashes in and out of the branches;
the moles tunnel underground unimaginably slowly, humming as they
    never have—
the glittering bees lift off from the bark of the trees unmoving beneath them;

and the sky, over the echoes of canyons and silence of caves,
retreats, as it might always, looking as if it is that sky into which released
    things are bound to rise—

into which if they make a bee-line, it is either with will-lessness or
    mindlessness.

MI RITROVAI

Here I was refound by a dark self;
My self was found by a darker self, obscure.
I was not one self, but made of wood

Within this wood—not single, but multiplied
On into darkness. No way to see for rest,
For all the trees, for all the terza rima.

A tree grows in the wood—what would you have me
Do? They all diverge into the darkness,
Dive into darkness, urge to obscurity.

How could one do anything but fall
Into a swoon, *svanire*? One cannot
Stand this, one cannot stand in the middle

Of this. And then I was found out by an
Obscure greeting—*salve*—strange advice
From something dark and savage that nonetheless

Spoke of salvage, through the loss, darkly.
Mi ritrovai per una selva oscura.
I back myself to the edge of a dark shelf.

Man hands on misery to man, it deepens—
So much deepens that one cannot stand
Here, in the middle of this mirror trove.

REFLECTING POOL

I was born in a city with a reflecting pool,
Clover-leaves, traffic circles, bridges like laces
Criss-crossing the river, on-ramps and off-ramps,
A bright white dome, and not far from the dome,
A train station and a botanical garden.
Riots I didn't see, ruin I did. The zoo I heard
In my sleep from my crib, a roaring alongside.
Maple helicopters. Marco Polo in the pool.
Camellias by the backdoor, dandelion wine
Brewing in the tub. Blue-jays in the side-yard,
Dive-bombing the cat. Pansies we picked
For the pinch-necked vase. Pale, looming hydrangeas
Bigger than your head. The Fuller brushman.
Locust buzzing by the front path. My right wrist
Gone through the glass panel of the downstairs door.
Peace roses, pine sap. Pearly accordion wheeze.
We made a four-leaf clover by gluing on a leaf
With Elmer's glue and believed in the luck we made.

THE CROSSING, 1969: USS UNITED STATES

What if you went to the movies and they were home?
The swimming pool's inside, where you can't sink
And disappear; the ceiling veers, bobs down,
Squishes you to the surface. That other brink
Outside the pool room, out there on the deck,
That other infinite surface, infinite depth—

Won't hold tight for a close-up. Hurricane:
The room rocks and then resets in its frame.
The focus leaps, blurs, saws away from threat.
For fun, upstairs, your mother places a bet
On horse races on tape. When the waves rock,
All you can do is sleep as if under lock

And key. But I want to understand the ocean,
Get to it, in it, under it, not to wall
Myself away from it. The iron crib
Falls down, steeply, but I am not there,
Where my baby brother cries; he doesn't know
Enough to scare,

My mother, brothers, sisters, sick and low.
The iron crib in the ocean liner, itself
Picked up like a paper boat and slapped
And slammed. And yet I was right there
When my grandmother was thrown into the air
Out of the lower bunk; I slept and slept.

All day on deck we drew
Together, folding the paper, passing it on,
All but the links left hidden. We'd unroll
Bird's head. Gorilla body. Spotted giraffe
Stilt legs. After the fold, two pointy shoes
On teetering heels. Of course you couldn't choose

What to connect to. We watched the wake
Making an endless ribbon for old time's sake,
Unraveling over the waves like invisible thread.
But where was Daddy? Had he flown ahead?
We should be going down and not across—
This is no way to understand the loss.

The family rearranges, and the pain
Lies in knowing it won't be *this* again.
It could open up—but you can't find the seam.
You're stuck in that VW from the dream,
The one from the old ad, airtight underwater:
You're nobody's son or daughter,

No breathing room. You hold your breath and float
And wait for life to send a ransom note.

AFTER THE STORM

1.

There was a humming in the house all day;
The flood subsiding into dampness, vapor;
But now the sky is gathering into gray;
The Mind's descending into closet stupor;
Under the cloud's deep voice, the Heart sinks deeper;
The Soul won't answer as the cardinal warbles;
And the water drags down the air like a sack of troubles.

2.

Where can they go, the things that live outdoors?
The ground despairs after nightlong destruction;
The grass is smeared and wrenched—and while it pours
The raccoon and three pups race in distraction
Toward and away from the house, and the opossum
Weaves, despairs, and worries through the mud
Some groove the water's worn; all things are flood.

3.

I was a Prisoner, my flood indoors;
I saw the hare outside, flattened with fear;
I heard the woods and distant waters roar
Even when they would still, sad as before;
The unstill season veined my heart with care;
The present moment cracks the present torment
As lightning downs the pine—not punishment

4.

But chance. Not punishment at all. How late
The light in minds that can no further go;
As low as we have sunk in our sad state
This slow solution lifts us—weary, slow,
And wavering with the evening. Even so,
What rises from torn root and residue,
Releasing resin, tastes both sharp and true.

5.

The wren inspects the ground beneath the pine;
Alert at the edge of the farthest bed, the deer
Acknowledges my presence. No design
Affords us these companions. We are here
In the green world by accident together—
Each day is accidental—accident
All friends, heart's bliss, and peace and nourishment.

6.

My whole life I have ached for happy thought
As if I were a prisoner in a flood
As if all needful things must still be sought
Outside myself. How bright and far the good
Flares in the lightning, seams and veins that should
Feed and inform the earth, and yet the pine
Is riven to the root. That charge is mine.

7.

What is thought? The Marvellous is human,
Even when sleeping deep beneath the word,
Beneath the river that a silly woman ·
Watches and would follow. Unknown bird
Another poet wrote about who heard
You singing questions, sing into eternity
Of accidental happiness and sanity.

THE WILD TURKEYS

Outside my kitchen window, Gambier

His eyes, from the unchanging gray, end-of-winter trees
suddenly light up, light suddenly upon
something particular. What is it he sees
that is not tree, not gray? The world taking on

motion as two, then seven, and then a flock of wild
turkeys, convening: two dozen sauntering, flaunting
improbable wingspreads and dignity—bigger than the child,
wiggly, transfixed. Something haunting,

always, unheimlich *and* homely—the scary human
scale of the birds, winged shoulders, one beaked head
slowly turning as they move slowly on
away from my son, sight, the now empty yard.

TODAY'S PUBLIC GARDEN

In Boston, the sky will be red tonight
while you die. The accountants cover their keyboards with plastic
cases and close their eyes while thirteen ducks
who have been bickering over breadcrumbs on the pond
in the Public Garden, today's Public Garden, in the new millennium, bury
their beaks under their wings without a sound.

Under the red roof, one house rejects
coats of paint. The renovators hacking at your neighbor's gutter
know everything there is to know about death. Your neighbor
holds her face in her hands, which are wet
as the rutted driveway by the renovator's van. She gives
you no thought, you are at work. And in a funny way, she's right.

You are working on dying in the Boston Public Garden. Oh,
what does it matter, the renovators can do nothing
with feathers. And Boston comes right down to the ground
in bricks. At the bottom of the pond, the light
is sour cherry, bitter tears of a girl
in a restaurant full of smokers. The iron benches

break your teeth, blankly, black. You will never
lie down under that ceiling, sirens
or no, workers hurriedly stripping
the old roofing from the frame in sheets.

Your neighbor doesn't know what she knows, she guesses
you're unrolled like bolts of satin over the skyline. Yes,

everything of how you work to escape this death.
She guesses what's in front of you, the bone white
horizon, the shadow of the boulder
where you closed in such a slow luxurious purple, her eyes
lidded like yours. The streetcars' eyes
are blue, frantically blinking, a sister's. Your neighbor shuts up.

Don't let anything touch you, because you
are not a child. You are older than that.
You are so old you think whatever you
don't want, the afterlife won't want either. Children
on the playground don't mind the grit of sand on their knees.
Swinging was work, you learned it; you

have to lunge into the sky where it resists.
The music you heard this morning inside
your neighbor's window dies in the ear of a duckling. You are so old
you don't know how hard it will be to lie down
on the bench, which never has room
for your brain. So when you clench your teeth,

you never guess the streetcar will speed between them
like an explosion, streaking your cheeks with red lights
and all its rain. But death is dumb, death wants
to get away *now*, and who knows why
as your teeth unclench, the children climb out
of the sandbox and head for the T-station, who knows why

the woman on hospice care in Boston dreamed
death was a balloon and pursed
her lips. And your neighbor, convinced, held
the beam and pilasters gleaming white
up to the new roof, as if she would stand there
forever in bright sun, so finally who cares what you do?

SHORT SHRIFT

Life's stirred up strife in the city center: strong thighs
pumping stronger, right and left hands insist
on unhinging each other in the heat.
Life dynamites my heart like a green leaf.
Oh, pay it no heed: it won't hold water.
I'm thrown out like a ball into the blue—
to the same old cost—but somehow I care less.

Life, you bastard,
                              you think you're so tough.
But before the last fuck I'll leave you, you can't guess
how my goodbye hits home: one wild pitch
dropped. One day, just nothing:
crowd's air cut off mid-roar. One last thrust
reduced to synecdochic cynicism—now, no news
is goodness, nothing tops the inexpressibility topos:
Life's undone in short shrift, lets down its blank
endpaper over me; yet no page abhors
airlessness, and no page abhors the red
cover clamped down on it like a mouth on white skin.

Two: How I Fell

A world who would not purchase with a bruise?
— John Milton, *Paradise Lost* (x.500)

HOW I FELL
& HOW IT FELT

At the movies, in my suede boots, like a fawn in the dark
startled by the lights, I fall; down the stairs vertiginous steep
I fall all week—and still fall, and still bark
and bloody my shin, and I am still asleep.

Or no, moving from Cheer, to Joy, to All,
I fall like a cumbersomely breaking sack
of groceries in the parking lot. Why call
for help, game hens, why hope for something back?

The "sorry's" go by me, like the jaunty sparrows
pecking the llama's grain. From a mother's sleep
I fell into such a state—the slings and eros
of outrageous fortune—I could weep

as Ash (our hero) now begins to weep
vast shining cartoon tears for the beloved
Pokemon who's died. But tears are cheap
as movie tickets. Everyone is moved

uniformly. I just feel it more
in my right shin. I bet there'll be a scar.

DAY OF NEEDS

I need a form—vertical? horizontal?
(from the side, or full-frontal?)
suicidal, or just mental?
or (I'm thinking toothache) dental?

I need a form—elaborate? simple?
(neither gap-toothed grin, nor dimple)
spare or (spare me) ample?
Would you like a free sample?

I need a form—try Chinese menu?
(intimate or public venue?)
loony bin, I've already been—you
think I'm trying to lose or win you?

I need a form—for neither/either
both/and friendly/heavy breather
down to earth and lost in ether
(oh brother)

I need a form—for what I need
some alphabet to write & read
(first see-saw, then gone to seed)
(don't plead)

I need a form—for I don't know
any more than the next guy, oh
next best, next to nothing, no
news is good, or make it so

I need a form like a hole in my head
my heart, my sole, my empty bed
the books that I've already read
& day-old bread

Whatever form of need you take
(or knead & bake)
can't have your cake
& eat it. Ache.

THE BODY IS A DISENCHANTING THING

is a disenchanted thing,
  like the rust in a
gasket ring
    encrusted by mud
      become undifferentiated crud.
Like Godzilla stomping New York City;

like the medicine ball
  as a butt; or the
worm's dirt-drawl
    of spun slime, the body
      charging ahead as if it could see,
hurtles and lurches every which way.

Oh, how deaf to the future
  it can't hear despite
its chuff and chirr.
    Like the skyscraper's rise,
    false enterprise,
because torqued by undermining imposture,

it is the fault of
  weak disenchantment. It
is like the shove-
    l mouth slowed by
    dirt; the future's why;
it's a foolish consistency.

It slobbers buckets, slobbers
   the remorse, the bruise,
the heart oozes
            from its guts—if the heart
            has guts; it has to start
ejection. It's ash in the shovel-mouth's

sludge; in the
   drudging persistences
of the sacked city.
      Confusion hammers
      its unconfusion to doubt; it's
not some virgin's wish that has to change.

WORDS

Words: the world's detritus, instant's ash,
        Mere human spit and sweat, dust into dust,
        The literal body, flesh worn out on flesh,
The faithless ricocheting gutter-blast;
A mighty engine's burps, the good man's gas
        Backfiring, and the hungry gut's great chord,
        The universe reduced to something less,
Cacophony unmarked, unheard, unfeared;
Hardness, and strife, and woe, and hate, all curst,
        Debased offal, sadness of the worst,
        Hell tricked out in costume, whores undressed,
The murky way, the bawd of Paradise,
        Sirens in the cross-walk, blood on blood,
A sea of stench; and nothing understood.

WHAT IS IT LIKE TO BE A BAT?

It will not help to try to imagine that one has webbing on one's arms,
which enables one to fly around at dusk and dawn catching insects in
one's mouth; that one has very poor vision, and perceives the surrounding
world by a system of reflected high-frequency sound signals; and that one
spends the day hanging upside down by one's feet in an attic. Insofar
as I can imagine this, it tells me only what it would be like for ME to behave
as a bat behaves. But that is not the question. I want to know what it's like
for a BAT to be a bat.
—Thomas Nagel

The bat in the moral philosophy exam woke up
the blonde from his study group,

falling asleep beside him (half-open blue
book barely scribbled in). *Act so the law*

of your actions a universal law would be able to become.
Alas, the Kant question was all she'd done.

He'd done more while she slept than she'd ever do.
Blinking, half taking in. *The dream was true—*

the test already begun, testing that never stops.
That look is what he kissed her for, her lips—

he laughs when he tells this part of the story later—
her lips clenched shut. (The nights she'd stayed

working to give back the words he'd say.
The hot bright light she'd carefully turned away.)

I can tell you this. No bat ever wasted time on
wondering what it was like to be a human.

MORTAL COIL

I started to write a poem called "Skin," about skin—

about snakes, snakeskins out in the toolshed: shed
vellum, opalescent. I touched them. Contact, tact

and disconnection. What it means to slough

out from the inside of something that is you
until you're gone from it: how you still see

snakes when the snake is gone. One six-foot skin

stays stretched out over the cross-cut saw; nobody
hurts here; held untorn, eased out of. How

that zig-zag helped you out of something, nicked

a threshold ridge across which you held yourself
half back and heaved half forward, or inched, or hunched

or rasped, or, unbunched, shuffled off to Buffalo . . .

But it's not finished. The husks haunt—who goes here?
Who's gone? What's left to touch or be touched by,

touched back? And there is something contagious, yes—

is it some worry what was lost mattered more,
what stays matters less? Or else, that we most know

ourselves as creatures in that state of friction

(tangle of bed-clothes, clothes on the bed), and must
always be skin to skin in the muddle, in the middle

of rubbing ourselves out, or into kindling, some kindness,
humidity, cruelty, some kind of human mess?

IN THE NIGHTS OF CACOPHONY

not in the nights before creation, but after
       Eden; when static crackled, and sound was
thick, not as in thickets
       riddled with snakes/hoots/lightning/vines; but because
of statistics; fifty-seven clicks & flickering channels

pitched to the galaxy, saturation was a chattering
       of the particular, outgoing messages
from answering machines; now it is all
       we have and then some; or does the sweet cool hum
of fridge and flourescent that sang "home" hold its own? It was never

about anything more than itself, the familiar. Read
       to me; family is not a game, now drop
everything. Silence.
       No thing, no song. Simplicity,
though, that whistles in the dark, and never

notices itself to be the benison it is, flutes high
       and low, not to guide us with some chirpy
dicta that acceptance
       will contain loss and that no
lie bleats and blares. On the tip of the tongue, what is plain is about

to change—singing in the inmost heart of the final
        tiny lies. All of it is silent, all of it
is about to fall silent, is any of it
        clamorous in the air? In the strong-lunged, force-
ful goodbyes, the megaphone and all the media, we have the tritest

single-mindedness, some think, thank god. Deception is no Gog
        and Magog, no formless chaos. It up and does. The moon
shudders in the cosmos like a gong. And it is so long gone, the silence after
        the signing off, out of hearing, out of here.

HIGH TIME

This high won't wear off till late afternoon.
In the drift of drowsiness, in the silt: sweet sift.
It's as if we'd been fired by fantasies

and these first flakes were the foreshadowings,
the fault-lines of an underground unease
we can't ward off for all the salt

in the deep blue sea or butterflies in China.
This high sizzles on the skin, as if the mind
weren't flicking its jaded switches behind the screen.

Let cool be cool, and then let dry run dry.
You don't forget the heartache in the high—it turns
us on, then turns its back on us. No idea escapes

itself, which is to say, we don't escape.
So each night's drought may dry our tears to salt,
but day breaks nonchalant toward the next high.

BRUISE

Music should never be harmless

More the near rhyme of deluge and damage
than the whole damn deal.

Error-aurora in azure, the leisurely surge
of submerged blue surfaceward—a blush

wondering under cool flesh what was heard
or hurt, hooded. Who did it want, whole

lush seepage of sound? *Hush.*

O risen from longing as lung and a prayer
let go & lunged for & O irrevocable,

cable cut, plunged. Song as receptacle
of no damage that is not reciprocal.

Not the eye-rhyme of injure and insure:
ashore unhurried, not unheard. *Inhere.*

ODE

After Horace, Ode I.9

Waiting, sleek hulks sheathed in ice, then dark.
The runways, sheathed ice rivers. Logan's closed,
immobilized; night closes down on trees
and freeways: friezes of abandoned cars.

Long gone the stragglers wading hip-deep drifts
toward home. Turn up the heat; and, like that, yes,
unwrap the Christmas Grand Marnier that slow
as some thing melting seems to warm the glass.

Leave to the gods all else. And if they launch
huge battling storm fronts, bitter turbulence
over the Great Lakes, they may yet relent
and sweep the Cambridge sidewalks with warm rain.

Or not. So what if colder morning brings
ice, the snow plows grinding through the gray
salt and fog. Don't think about age or time,
not now. Think about love, think about girls singing,

sunlight on water, a picnic. Consign the rest
to the plow. This day is just this day—so clear
your desk, you fool! It's not too late for whispers,
for hurried arrangements in the not-yet night—

listen to that laugh, the laugh that gives
away something she's thinking in the dark
under the covers where she turns and twists
the telephone cord around one pretty wrist.

AFTER WORDS

We do not tire entire. Sad in the middle
Of sadness's inadequacy, we fiddle
And burn out, softly. Life in fear of life
Makes matter matter less, and less of strife
And breathing softly. Some things we'll never know.
Long distance doesn't care. We come and go.

FACING THE JUDGE, AT THE ALTAR

Why should we do this? What good is it to us? Above all, how
can we do such a thing? How can it possibly be done?
—Sigmund Freud

I.

My name is Jenny Scott; I found my end
at the Textile Museum, on Embassy Row,
on S. Street. What my father didn't know
couldn't hurt me. What the government
didn't know could hurt him. What is kind
in institutions is impersonal,
also, what is cruel. Marriage is all
it is cracked up to be. The carousel
down on the Mall will stand still for a price.
I never got to ride the jeweled horse.
I learned to make a puppet from old spools;
I learned to heat the powdered glass in pools
rimmed with silver wires: cloisonné,
"little prisons." And I learned to dye.
I miss my arts and crafts lessons, release
and discipline combined, their steadiness.

2.

Daddy, I never loved him as I love you,
But love wouldn't let me alone. And now what's done
is cracked and cooling like the empty kiln,
oh heart. These days I pretty much behave
in Gambier: Wednesdays I put out the trash,
Thursdays, recycle. Leaves flare up, the nights
edge in, skunks brazen it out, the air is rich
enough to stop a horse in its tracks. I get
a trampoline, protected by a net.
Daddy, I'll be OK. Some things don't die.
The tuner will come fix the broken key.

3.

The invisible altar holds as true as steel.
We still hold on to what we couldn't do
in fear, in love. When no one can hold still
in the next breeze,
and the servants of the air rise up
into their wings, to hover and forgive
the living who go on living everywhere,
then may these minds—mother and child and practiced penitent—
easily unwind their fretful knots,
and breathe as if they were not made of thoughts.

I KNOW WHY YOU WENT TO MEMPHIS, UH HUH

I went to the southern cities for the waters
and they gave me beer; I went out for some air
and they gave me beer. I went to the southern cities
for the delay and they gave me delay and more
delay down to the river through the rasping
grass, I lay back into the roughness, down
I went to the southern cities. They took away
my vowels, Mommy, they sealed my fate with a lick
of hot sauce on each wrist, my ribs, my twisty
ribbons, ribonucleic acids and balms
got soaked, soaked it way in. And it's all in the way
you're twisted. As in, for *balms* I mistyped *blams*,
then *blames*, then *Alabamans*. In the south
(don't say "down there") they took away my need
to know, they took away every little thing
that was too sharp, my tiny nail
scissors, but they held onto their guns.
The southern city was the same walled city everywhere,
the same wild city everywhere. Some things
can be willed, and some things can't. The dream that split us
into three since there was too much hurt
for two—its slip-knot, triangle, delta, meaning
change, now *scratch* the record—how in that dream
I wanted the tiny scissors to cut him out
in little stars—my eyes, I couldn't find

where she had put the scissors, *in his back?*
In mine? She shook her head. And I went south,
shoveling, and shut down. My tiny mouth
don't open enough for a vowel, clamped down so hard
on a rib, on somebody's rib. This sauce ain't bad.

CULTURAL INSTRUCTIONS: SPRING

I am proceeding in ignorance and by conjecture.
—Ezra Pound, "The Chinese Written Character as a Medium for Poetry"

The moon is a dirty bulb, sun-disc with horns,
bright feathers flying, short-tailed bird, and "like"
is a woman's mouth. She mouths "sun-sky," "sky-broom,"
sweeping motion of snow, cloud roof, a cloth
over falling drops. A crooked tree, and "like"
is a woman's breast. Man and spoon under plants,
as if for planting bulbs, "as if" becomes flowers
at the height of a man's head. How the man now tries
toward the woman's mouth: knife fire of the sun,
fire over moving legs of a man, sun bright.
Mouth hook. In love with fire, heart girl descending
through. Archaic balance and melting pots.
Erect sun, legs running. Bent knuckle, bent
object revolving around a pivot. A "garden"
is "blend," is "pace," is "in the midst," and rain
in the midst of a court, lit by a dirty bulb,
a court ransacked, dug up. See "high above"
and bend around a pivot. Jewel. Plain man
and dog. Weeds—plants cover knife—growing
not as if things that must be destroyed.
Fragrance, specifically given, fragrance "as if"
from a distance. Like sun (spoon) now under growing
tree. Brush sun underwood, brush burying sun.

WHO'S COUNTING?

Light almost gone.
Let the bird who knows too much keep telling it all.
Let the retriever at home sit up and wait
faithfully, as always.
Who cares if the bird never sleeps, or how long it warbles
steadily, on and on.
The news of the world will never be exhausted,
never, in all those melodies,
tired or told.

Velvet night, benevolent, forgetful;
shadows infiltrating shadow-bodies,
shadowy limbs,
pouring double velvet along the veins.
Surely the bird has flown. How sweet the tune.

———

The golden retriever cowers at the gate.
Her owner's voice falls, lightly—
"There, there, I'm home,"
but she wants to understand what she's done wrong.
She cringes and grovels,
pleading in the dirt.

She seems ready to take the blame for anything.
She and the bird don't know what to ask first,
everything's up in the air,
and no one to answer.
—Last night weighs on today so heavily!
(A life I must find easy to let go.)

Three: Counter-Amores

HAPPY HOUR

"Happy hour" in harsh winter.
You hunch, tense, at your desk.

Lights off in the outer office, the terminal glow
parodies the blue light of a diner

reduced to a blue plate, like the leftover
dish still in the sink at 2 a.m.

I don't care if it's light or dark,
I can't wait.

I want to start saying your name; I'm buttoned up,
pinned up, wound up, just to make you

work hard at the work at hand, and not
fast enough to stop me, either,

God, from grabbing at our clothes; too much is hidden.
If I fight to give it away, I fight

with all my heart.
Defeat is hard. I will betray you.

And if you were at last to lie—human, flawed—
next to me on this pillow,

shoulders and arms relaxed in sleep, exposed,
helpless, even—how could I endanger

that easy breathing, how send these light fingers
wandering down your belly under the covers?

Who's perfect?
Merciless, I'd attack in an instant,

why dream I'd let you rest? Wake up! This night
is more than ours—I swear this night is mine.

ALL'S FAIR

All's fair; I think I'll let you go—too small
to keep. And I don't care whether you call
me back or not. Perhaps I've aimed too low
(below the belt); I think I'll let you go.

You wouldn't last a minute as my slave,
would you? (Oh, you don't know what you have
to lose. Besides, I know your middle name,
computer passwords, your recurring dream

or nightmare that these secrets you record,
that seem secure behind the darkened screen,
open to other keyboards, every word
winks like the girl you hoped would wait unseen.)

Love has nothing to do with it. I take
what I want and lie about it later
and blame *you*, sweetheart. Oh, I take the cake
and let them eat it, too—and that's the matter,

isn't it? Eat and be eaten. Who survives
I might at last consent to keep as slave.
Might. My sister Fates—one spins, one weaves,
one *cuts* the thread. I do not grieve

ever. What's dead is dead. Leave me alone
and I'll get back to writing something else.
You'll be forgotten when they read this poem:
it's only better-than-average sex that *sells*.

The Lady of the Tapestries can touch
the horn of the animal she loves so much,
touch anchoring the world that she holds dear
and lets go, praying, *à mon seul desir*.

Tapestries unravel. Beasts are dumb.
I think I'll let you go. (Or let you come.)

PROOF

Than brandished fire yet will I prove more strong—
I burn unshaken, burn and die day-long.
The hooked fish, torn, must learn to slip the bait
Teasing the hook let go before too late.
Not with you, but against you, love, I bruise
My mouth, manage myself such pain I choose.
I will this torment as I can't will love
From you or me—what can a body prove?
Though neither yours nor love's, still I'm a slave.
Untie me from myself—I'm yours to have.

THAT WAY

It's wrong for him to hit her in that way
across the face—completely wrong. That way
madness lies. When Malkovich hits Kidman
in Campion's *Portrait of a Lady*, man
turns beast. But Gilbert Osmond is a beast
to Isabel when he is least a beast,
when he refuses to display his rage
at her; he is most cruel when his rage
is coldest, softest, quietest—and she
cannot fight back, can hardly even speak
or move. His tone, when he at last does speak,
is grave, sincere, with all the subtlety
of the subtlest threads that tether her, subtlety
so much more cruel than outright violence—
that's why it's wrong, that outright violence.
If he had hit her, that would let her go—
it would explode in her and let her go.
When he hauls off and hits her he is changed
just as surely as Lycaon is changed
into a wolf by the force of his emotion,
and Actaeon to a deer by *his* emotion—
choked with rage the tyrant cannot speak,
the breathless, panicked victim cannot speak—
the body registers rage and fear past words—

and Isabel and Osmond are past words,
where words can't reach, about to force the story
to the bursting point: this is the story
that tells us, now that violence exists,
it exists the way the real body exists—
to free us from the things we cannot say—
the body exists to free us in that way.

COUNTER-AMORES   I.14

TO DYE FOR

You could ask me to dye my hair,
But if I were to do it,
It wouldn't be to make you care.
There wouldn't be much to it.

White blonde when I was young,
Ash-blonde now I am old,
Or chestnut gray, still long,
A raggedy, dull gold.

The wiry whites refuse
To lie down on my head—
The news of time is news
I wouldn't have unsaid.

How I looked as if I'd just
Hauled myself out of bed—
Hair all tousled, mussed
My boyfriend's girlfriend said.

I hadn't slept with him.
Anyway, she was married,
Older (though now I am
Older than she was). Buried,

The hatchet. After death
They say your hair still grows.
And what grows after love
Is dead, the dyer knows.

I'M BAD

I'm bad—but I behave—I contradict
myself—I never do what I depict.
I don't have morals, but I still live chaste;
I write the worst so it won't go to waste.
I don't lie down—but still a girl can lie
on paper—to remember someone by.
In sanity—a clean, well-lighted place—
I write things you won't read upon my face.
Brides and virgins need their privacy;
invite a crowd—there's nothing here to see.
(Honestly? This name was never mine—
if it becomes notorious, that's fine
by me—how many times has he had sex
since he became my once and future ex?
Let him assume I never sleep at night—
not that what keeps me up's this need to write.)

Nuns fret not at their convents' narrow rooms.
I'm not ashamed to fret. The wide world looms
so I lie down, under the fretful covers
and fret with all my dearly faulty lovers
who wander fully clothed at some remove
of minds and miles—they don't guess that they love,
or the proximity of lip & tongue

the infinite ways that we've devised to come,
the things I say he's never failed to say,
the mess we made of the sheets the other day.
Am I then so dishonest when I lie
all unashamed, because what haven't I
done with you—all that we haven't done
exposed here to the full light of the sun.

I lie with you, I lie for all to see,
enjoy such lying as allowed to me.

Material proof—what kind of evidence
(DNA, denial)—that's the president's
problem. If I say you're here with me
then here you are. And here. And heresy
the claim a heart might need more proof than this
or body confirmation of heart's bliss.
It's life when I protest what we have done
and through real veins I feel the hot blood run.
Then you, whom I can't have, I love as real
as life and twice as natural, I feel
you in my bones. I've nothing to declare
except my self—I'm duty free—I swear
I'm ninety-nine and forty-four percent pure
guilt—I only wish my guilt secure.
Could we do something that I couldn't say
or trust to paper? Dear, I'd seize the day.

COUNTER-AMORES   III.5

A DREAM

"My mind is like a CD-ROM in a computer—like a quick-access videotape.
But once I get there, I have to play that whole part." She could not just focus,
for instance, on the cradling of the animal in its last moments; she had to play,
in memory, the entire scene, from the animal entering the chute and progressing
steadily ("no fast forward, it takes about two minutes") until the death of the
animal and its collapse, after its throat has been cut.
—Oliver Sacks, on Temple Grandin, in *An Anthropologist on Mars*

I wish there were a white cow, and a crow,
some beast that I don't know—

I wish there were a black bull, and a dove,
a lion starved for love

haunch-deep in the waters of the stream
without a name, the stream

aswim with symbols, flowing allegory,
I wish there were a story

needing an interpreter to uncover
what matters when it's over

someone reconstructing, without siding
with me, what I'm hiding

from myself because that's what I ask of art—
that it let me eat my heart

and have it, too—I say I wish that you
had not been there as you

have never been with me, and that when I
ran for the ramp to try

to skate away, ramp curiously designed
to pitch me down inclined

and forward looking up I looked at her
she looked at me *I wish I were*

not I, you not you, she not she your wife
and this a dream, not life.

COUNTER-AMORES   II.1

BACK AGAIN

These lines write themselves. I push away
from the shapes they make. They want to say
what I don't want. The more I race—erase—
to try to get away, the more I face

backward. Read me, you who have let go
the need to nail down some truth in the past,
and take me with you. Cupid doesn't know
the trouble I've seen, doesn't know the cost.

It's not about lost love; hate doesn't learn
how not to burn, and he will not get lost.
If there's no god to make my case to, why
do I keep trying, keep framing the *I*—

the irony? Away and back I swerve
to irony, God *Irony*, I serve
my cup of rage—and if you serve me right,
to you I'd give my word, my words, I'd write

and write the moon back in the sky, that gold
companionable face (since to reflect
is to be patient and benevolent, to hold
one's judgment in abeyance, recollect

what haste and hate might poison and destroy
and so think twice), or else I'd write away
all stars and planets, empty out the sky
of anything but free air. God *Irony*,

I'd write your clean, sweet name on every door,
and if the door's alarmed I'd write it twice,
and if the door's ajar, I'd break the jar
and write it on each shard, on the black ice

sheeting the highway, on the winter sky,
and everywhere would read: God *I*, God *I*.

NEWS FLASH
My love's fire is absent.

I'm at Irvine, here in Orange County:
        which spreads out, mall after contagious mall,
under the winter rains. The exuberant pine tree
        flaunts its ponytail-like needle-fall.

Mud torrents down the drive at Malibu,
        down the hillside roller-coaster fire
swept bare last month. "It's worth it for the view,"
        he says, rubbing his wispy chin. Desire

hurtles over the last retaining wall, and over the coastal
        highway, where the wild surf, too, goes postal.

COUNTER-AMORES I.1

ARMS ABOUT YOU

The bells rang "la bella vita" into the Roman air,
           and all I wanted was a room somewhere
to fall in love and write about it, lightly. Now
           "Ciao, bella" modulates to "Bella, ciao":
a sweet and bitter tune to move this March along
           while *bella, horrida bella* weights the song
down, more heavily down. How the bell's clamor
           shocks and awes the air like hammering armor,
ringing in the ear. Sound bites the sense away,
           bites the ear that heeds it, sees the day
bitten down to the quick, down to the clenched jaw
           that knows there is another use for "awe."

And I was sick with love for the bark of the sycamore,
           layers stripping back to some live core,
like an Ovid in reverse, the girl trapped in the tree
           struggling for release, simultaneously
chased, grasped, and unclasped, torn and untorn:
           to see into that bark was to be reborn
into another world—to see the name "amor"
           written into the heart of the sycamore.
But now the mottled ivory, dove-gray, olive-gray
           is given back to me a different way:
as military camouflage. And I can't make the war
give me back myself, or the sycamore.

WHAT SHE THOUGHT

What's poetry? Is it the fruits and vegetables and
marketplace of Campo dei Fiori, or
the statue of the martyr there?
[…] The truth
is both, it's both I said.
—Heather McHugh, "What He Thought"

But if this is an idea of truth as inclusive,
it's bigger than both marketplace and statue—
it has to be at least as big as the billboard
towering over both of them: don't ask me
what it's selling: there's a sexy, tight-skirted
ass being grabbed by the right hand of a life-size
wooden dummy the woman is carrying
(with surprising lightness) under her left arm,
his eyeless head peering around her left hip
(her head, of course, is cropped out of the frame).
I don't know if it is an Italian
habit to see this or to ignore this, but I
fixate on the way the dummy's fingers
individually press, like Pluto's in Bernini's
"Rape of Proserpina," into her right
buttock. But more than that, it's poetry
in the *trompe l'oeil* billboard framing this one,
mimicking the real façade behind it:
ochre stucco, gray shutters, cream-colored trim—

and from three *trompe l'oeil* windows, rainbow
PACE flags hang down, just like the ones
on adjacent buildings, except that these
don't flutter in the wind. And if something
smells a bit fishy here, it's because the best
view is from this corner of the market
where the fish seller's large brown hand is gutting
the white belly of an enormous fish,
then tossing it into a bin. I'm close enough
to hear the knife crick-cracking its way through
the next fish, to see his left hand up in under
the gills, the white "flesh / packed in like feathers"
(not unlike the Madonna del Parto, by Piero
della Francesca, the way the neat white seams
in the front of her dress are beginning to pull apart).
He heaves that fish into the bin as well.
Elaine Scarry says that beauty prompts a copy
of itself, that generation is unceasing:
when the eye sees someone beautiful, the whole body
wants to reproduce the person, to do
justice to the seen. Directly under
the dummy billboard, there's a booth where one
can buy peace flags, along with diverse aprons
advertising fourteen shapes of pasta,
kinds of cheese, Italian wines, or featuring
trompe l'oeil torsos: nearly naked except
for black lace lingerie and garter belt,
or else full-frontal David. We're the species
that copies things because we love a joke.
We love the way a joke holds out the idea
of how things ought to be and *uses* that against us.

(One has to think the first joke went like this:
God made us in his image.) At the moment
everything in the Campo seems to tremble
with the heat, activity, and too many visual
rhymes, games, silly questions—because we are
the species always asking questions, just
to try them out—I have to remember what
I came for: tomatoes. *Pomodori.*
And my vegetable guy knows, without my asking,
to add the usual *due foglie di basilico.*
What's meaning? What's meaningful? Silly, but then
I'm thinking about the relationship *(folie à deux)*,
between those leaves of basil and a basilica,
and then I'm remembering that "silly,"
because it takes us past the bounds of reason,
comes from *Seele,* comes from the word for soul.

UNFINISHED BUSINESS

Oblivious boy, continue to ignore me.
Do I write less than when you are before me?

I'll keep writing just to bring you back.
How could I work if I weren't faced with lack?

Friends and advisors who are keeping score,
My book's not finished yet, and we are still at war.

Whether I write from Washington or Rome,
My homework is disheveled, and my home.

The cities are too heavy, poems too light.
I'll write about the tree frogs in the night

Whose legions thrill and trill when dusk comes on.
Anonymous neighbors. Singing on and on.

NOTES

The quote from Margaret Talbot on p. v comes from the *New Yorker* article, "Birdbrain: The Woman Behind the World's Chattiest Parrots," published May 12, 2008.

"After the Equinox": This poem was written after a talk given by Sidney Wade on translating Turkish poetry, and is dedicated to her.

"*Mi Ritrovai*": Readers will recognize the title and phrases within this poem from the opening of Dante's *Inferno*:

> Nel mezzo del cammin di nostra vita
> mi ritrovai per una selva oscura
> che la diritta via era smarrita.

If readers recognize, or think they recognize, words from other writers in this poem (or in other poems here), they are encouraged—but not required—to entertain such recognitions. "How I Fell & How It Felt," for example, was written with Randall Jarrell in mind (and ear). "Words," in a different way, draws from George Herbert. Poems offered out of gratitude for other beloved poems perhaps inevitably reinscribe their deepest debts.

"Facing the Judge, at the Altar": This poem shares its epigraph with James Wright's "At the Executed Murderer's Grave."

"Cultural Instructions: Spring": Ezra Pound, in his discussion of Ernest Fenollosa's work on the Chinese written character as a medium for poetry, devotes most of his attention to the role of ideograms in expressing nouns and verbs. But the working notes for these translations also include, among others, ideograms for "like" and for "as if," whose picture-characters have a connection harder to fathom as to the functions of those words. Under the eyes of a reader who knows little about the Chinese written language, the characters *in* these ideograms (for all kinds of words) begin—as they often do in stories—to lead double lives, not only in the author's sentences, but also in stories of their own. The title of this poem is taken from the White Flower Farms planting manual.

"Counter-Amores": The poems in this third section engage in call-and-response with Ovid's *Amores* (in versions by Guy Lee, A.D. Melville, and Christopher Marlowe). They are meant to stand on their own, but if they lead readers to these less familiar poems of Ovid's, so much the better. To counter Ovid here is to encounter him, to sit across a counter and to have words between us. Sometimes one finds oneself best in talking back. Ovid's elegiac couplets already talk back to themselves, with the second, shorter line in each pair falling away from and often undercutting the first. Readers who seek out the originals (or the translated versions) may see a perversity in the precise degree of countering Ovid here; for the writer, this discipline offered a contemporary analogue to the formal challenge of Ovid's couplets.

"Counter-Amores I.i: Arms About You": The march in question was the peace march in Rome, on February 15, 2003, where literally millions marched, from all over the country; although Berlusconi supported the war, the war did not have popular Italian support. My immediate companions in the march were one British and two Italian friends from the American Academy in Rome; they taught me the words to "Bella Ciao." It is a protest song—the song most widely sung by the crowds during the march—with a tune like a slower, graver "Darling Clementine." *Bella, horrida bella* are words that the Sybil offers Aeneas in the underworld: essentially, "wars, horrible wars." For Italians, the Iraq war started on March 20th—Ovid's birthday.

"What She Thought": The phrase "flesh / packed in like feathers" comes from Elizabeth Bishop's "The Fish." The Elaine Scarry work referred to here is *On Beauty and Being Just*.